3/25/19
$28 50

Becoming a Fly

by Grace Hansen

CHANGING ANIMALS

Abdo Kids Jumbo is an Imprint of Abdo Kids
abdopublishing.com

abdopublishing.com

Published by Abdo Kids, a division of ABDO, P.O. Box 398166, Minneapolis, Minnesota 55439.
Copyright © 2019 by Abdo Consulting Group, Inc. International copyrights reserved in all countries.
No part of this book may be reproduced in any form without written permission from the publisher.
Abdo Kids Jumbo™ is a trademark and logo of Abdo Kids.

052018

092018

THIS BOOK CONTAINS
RECYCLED MATERIALS

Photo Credits: Alamy, Animals Animals, iStock, Minden Pictures, Shutterstock

Production Contributors: Teddy Borth, Jennie Forsberg, Grace Hansen

Design Contributors: Dorothy Toth, Laura Mitchell

Library of Congress Control Number: 2017960559

Publisher's Cataloging-in-Publication Data

Names: Hansen, Grace, author.

Title: Becoming a fly / by Grace Hansen.

Description: Minneapolis, Minnesota : Abdo Kids, 2019. | Series: Changing animals |
    Includes glossary, index and online resources (page 24).

Identifiers: ISBN 9781532108167 (lib.bdg.) | ISBN 9781532109140 (ebook) |
    ISBN 9781532109638 (Read-to-me ebook)

Subjects: LCSH: Flies--Juvenile literature. | Animal life cycles--Juvenile literature. |
    Insects--Metamorphosis--Juvenile literature. | Animal behavior--Juvenile literature.

Classification: DDC 571.876--dc23

Table of Contents

Stage 1

All flies begin as eggs. Fly eggs look like small grains of rice.

4

5

A female fly lays around 75 to 150 eggs in a **batch**. She will lay up to 6 batches in her life.

She will lay her eggs in
dark, damp places.
These include rotting foods,
plants, and manure.

9

Stage 2

It only takes about a day for an egg to hatch. But the insect looks nothing like an adult fly. It is a **larva**!

11

A fly larva is also called a maggot. The maggot does not have any legs or wings. It cannot move very far.

13

Luckily, the female fly laid its eggs on something maggots love to eat! The maggot eats, grows, and **molts**.

15

Stage 3

The maggot **molts** one last time. Its skin becomes a hard, brown shell. This protects the maggot while it changes into an adult fly.

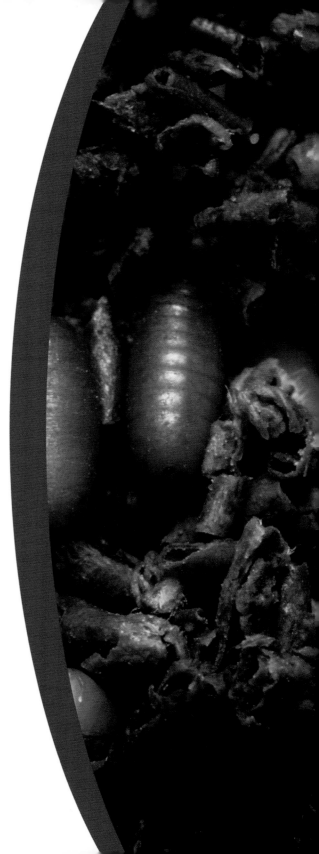

16

17

Stage 4

These big changes take around six days. When the fly is ready, it **emerges** from its shell.

19

Female flies will lay eggs after about two days. And the cycle will begin again!

21

More Facts

- Houseflies usually live 15 to 30 days.

- Female flies do not care for or protect eggs.

- If food is available, maggots double in size two days after hatching.

Glossary

batch – an amount of something that is made at one time.

emerge – come out.

larva – the early form of an insect that at birth or hatching does not look like its parents and must grow and change to become an adult.

manure – an animal's solid waste.

molt – to shed skin that will be replaced by new skin.

23

Index

Abdo Kids ONLINE

FREE! ONLINE MULTIMEDIA RESOURCES

Visit **abdokids.com** and use this code to access crafts, games, videos, and more!

Abdo Kids Code:

CBK8167